SOAP! SOAP!
DON'T FORGET THE SOAP!

For my home state, North Carolina, which will always be in my blood,
and for storytellers everywhere. Your tales are the seeds of culture.

T.B.

To Taylor in Livingston, e Tommaso a Bologna.

A.G.

SOAP! SOAP! DON'T FORGET THE SOAP!

An Appalachian Folktale

retold by Tom Birdseye

illustrated by Andrew Glass

Holiday House/New York

STORE

Up in the mountains of North Carolina, way back in Sassafras Hollow, there once was a boy with such a poor memory some say he'd forget his own name.

"Plug! Plug Honeycut!" folks'd yell when they saw him walk by.

Plug Honeycut would stop and look
around.
 "Plug! Hey, Plug! It's you being talked to,
Plug!"

Plug would take off his old floppy-brimmed hat. He'd scratch his head and think, think, think. "Plug?" he'd say. "*Plug*?"

But only after what seemed like forever would that forgetful boy finally remember that *he* was named Plug, and that someone was saying howdy-do to *him*. He'd wave real friendly, but right quick he'd lose track of why he was waving.

Because, you see, *no one* was as forgetful as Plug.
But Plug Honeycut's mama loved her only son.

Come one particular bath day, when she found she was out of soap, she sent him to the store with some money.

"Now don't forget, Plug," she said with the faith that only a mother could have. "Soap! Soap! Don't forget the soap!"

Plug smiled at his mama, and said he wouldn't forget—"No ma'am!" He lit out the door saying, "Soap! Soap! Don't forget the soap! Soap! Soap! Don't forget the soap!" to help himself remember.

Well, this worked mighty fine, at least until Plug got to the muddy old creek. Halfway over, though, balancing on a slippery stepping stone, Plug spied a big bullfrog and, just like that, he up and forgot about the soap.

Plug took off his floppy-brimmed hat, scratched his head, and thought, thought, thought. But that didn't help none. Because, as you're sure to remember, *no one* was as forgetful as Plug.

Just about then, an old woman came by on her way to a
quilting bee. She carefully put her foot on a stepping stone
and mighty near slipped and fell into the muddy old creek.
"Oooee!" she said. "That stepping stone's as slick as *soap*!"

Plug's eyes lit up. "SOAP!" he yelled. "Soap! Soap! Don't forget the soap!"

The old woman was so startled at the sound of Plug's voice, she plum lost her balance and fell—KERSPLAT—into the creek.

Mad as that made her, she reached up and pulled Plug in too, dunking him twice for good measure.

"What a mess I've become, but now you're one, too!" the old woman hollered. Then she climbed out of the creek and stomped off.

Plug hauled himself out and tried to remember what his mama had sent him to do. He even took off his hat, scratched his head, and thought, thought, thought. But, as you're sure to remember, *no one* was as forgetful as Plug. All he could think of was what the old woman had yelled. So down the road he went, saying just that: "What a mess I've become, but now you're one, too! What a mess I've become, but now you're one, too!"

It wasn't more than two bumps and a bend in the road later that Plug Honeycut came upon a boy who had tumbled tail past teakettle over his bicycle handlebars. He'd landed upside down in the blackberry brambles with his basket of eggs on his head.

And there came Plug, saying "What a mess I've become, but now you're one, too! What a mess I've become, but now you're one, too!"

This didn't sit too kindly with the boy in the blackberry brambles, who thought Plug was making fun of him. Up he jumped and grabbed Plug, cracking his one remaining egg on Plug's floppy-brimmed hat. Then he threw Plug into all those troublesome stickers.

"So there!" he hollered. "Look who's in a fix now!"

Poor Plug. Those thorns weren't gentle with his clothes or his hide, either. If he'd been a mess before, he was a *real* mess now. He untangled himself and crawled back out onto the road, but—of course—he couldn't remember then what he hadn't remembered before. Because, as you're sure to remember, *no one* was as forgetful as Plug.

So instead of saying "Soap! Soap! Don't forget the soap! Soap! Soap! Don't forget the soap!" off he went saying what he'd heard last instead: "Look who's in a fix now! Look who's in a fix now!"

Down the road a piece a tree had fallen on top of an unfortunate farmer's truck. Plug hobbled upon the scene, still saying "Look who's in a fix now! Look who's in a fix now!"

The farmer took it all wrong. He wasn't in the best of moods, what with a tree on top of his truck and all. And thinking Plug was making fun of him got him even more riled. He grabbed Plug by the collar . . .

. . . and marched him right over to the truck, where he made
Plug saw that tree up into firewood and load it in his truck.

"Nothing on top, and better off for it!" growled the farmer as he
drove away an hour later.

Poor Plug. By then he was covered with all manner of sawdust and sweat, and truck grease and grime—that besides the mud and the egg and the blackberry scratches. And he couldn't remember what his mama sent him out for, either. All he could recollect was what the farmer had said. So off he lit toward the town saying just that: "Nothing on top, and better off for it! Nothing on top, and better off for it!"

Land sakes alive! If Plug's troubles weren't enough, along came a man so bald on top the birds were blinded by the sun reflecting off his scalp. And there came Plug, saying "Nothing on top, and better off for it! Nothing on top, and better off for it!"

The bald man thought Plug was mocking him for his hairless head. He reached over and snared Plug quicker than a frog does a fly.

"Look a-here, you!" the bald man scolded. "I'm growing me a fine beard on my chin since I ain't got none on top! You could at least have said, 'You look nice with hair on your face!'" He was so mad, he pulled Plug's hat right down over his ears.

Poor Plug. He was covered with mud, egg, scratches, sawdust, sweat, grease, and grime, and now his hat was ruined. He started to cry and streaked it all with tears!

But, as you're sure to remember, *no one* was as forgetful as Plug. So as he went sniffling into town, he *still* couldn't recall what his mama had sent him for. Instead of saying "Soap! Soap! Don't forget the soap! Soap! Soap! Don't forget the soap!" he could only think of what the bearded bald man had hollered: "You look nice with hair on your face!"

And that was what he said—"You look nice with hair on your face! You look nice with hair on your face!"—to the mayor's wife.

Poor Plug! The mayor's wife was the prissiest lady in town, always fussing with her lipstick and such, and admiring herself in any mirror handy.

"Why, you!" she shrieked, and grabbed him by the ear. She shook him so hard, his eyeballs rattled. "I ought to wash your mouth out with *soap* for saying such a thing to me!"

At the sound of the word *soap*, Plug lit up like Methuselah's birthday cake. "SOAP!" he cried. "Soap! Soap! Don't forget the soap!"

Plug ran straight to the general store
and bought some soap.

Then he hotfooted it home, shouting to his mama, "Soap! Soap! Don't forget the soap!" (He was so proud! He'd remembered!) "Soap! Soap! Don't forget the soap!"

"Why thank you, dear," Plug's mama said. She looked him up and down. "I'd say soap is *just* what we need."

And from that day on—as you're sure to remember—Plug Honeycut never forgot a thing his mama told him . . . not ever again . . . for the rest of his life.

Library of Congress Cataloging-in-Publication Data
Birdseye, Tom.
Soap! Soap! don't forget the soap! : An appalachian folktale /
retold by Tom Birdseye ; illustrated by Andrew Glass
p.   cm.
Summary: A forgetful boy gets himself into trouble when he
repeats what each person he meets on the road says to him.
ISBN 0-8234-1005-6
[1. Folklore—Appalachian Region.]   I. Glass, Andrew, ill.
II. Title.
PZ8.1.B534sk   1993   92-11295   CIP   AC
398.2—dc20
[E]

ISBN 0-8234-1230-X (pbk.)